250
Things to
Do Before
You Turn
25

250 Things to Do Before You Turn 25

Tammy Mitchell

1. Own a passport.

Having a passport makes the world a whole lot smaller. Get one, keep it somewhere safe. You'll use it, trust me.

2. Learn to like yourself.

Part of growing up is learning to love the skin you're in, flaws and all. Practice loving yourself a little everyday. Be able to stand in front of your mirror, naked, and find five things you love about what you see. Be able to embrace yourself for who you are and you'll be 100% happier.

3. Get a diploma.

It doesn't have to be from a fancy Ivy League school but by 25, get the diploma you want and deserve whether it's your high school diploma or you're finishing up a Master's degree.

4. Attempt a "Man vs. Food" challenge.

Don't be discouraged if you don't finish and don't get sick if you do!

5. Don't run the heating 24/7 during the winter.

You'll learn quickly that keeping your apartment at a balmy 80 degrees in the winter time is going to end in a pretty hefty electric/gas bill. The same goes for air conditioning in the summer time.

6. Read an entire book series.

Whether it's three or thirty books, get sucked in and read them all.

7. Learn what good wine really is.

Sure, there's always going to be three buck chuck you can buy off the Walmart shelf but sometimes, you just want a nice glass of wine with dinner and that $3 bottle isn't going to cut it.

8. Additionally, learn what good beer is.

You may have enjoyed a few cases of "Natty Light" in your day but learn to appreciate different, more sophisticated types of beer.

9. Test drive your dream car.

Once you're over 18, you can test drive cars at dealerships. Before you turn 25, dress up so you look rich enough to buy your dream car and head on over to the lot. It'll be fun riding around in a car you can't really afford, even if it's just for a few minutes.

10. Perform 10 random acts of kindness in one day.

11. Go scuba diving.

Explore the world beneath the water's surface.

12. Apply for your dream job.

If you're tired of interning and earning well below what you think you should be earning, go ahead and apply for that dream job. It can't hurt to put in an application and even getting an interview and networking can do wonders for you in the long run.

13. Find your personal style.

You don't have to dress like everyone else. Find your own signature look and rock it.

14. Go on a blind date.

It might suck but it could turn out really well!

15. Take an art class with your friends.

Wine and design classes are really popular and great for a girls' night out.

16. Try new recipes.

Try a new recipe every week for a whole year.

17. Learn quality vs. quantity.

Sure, it's fun going on a Forever 21 shopping spree every month and walking out of the store with a huge bag of clothes for practically nothing. However, those clothes are cheap and won't last. Start investing in clothes that will last you years. The money you invest now will pay off later. You can still buy your cheap, trendy clothes (you're only 25!), just be sure to add in some nice, quality staples as well.

18. Grow an avocado tree from a pit.

There are tons of tutorials online for how to grow an avocado and the plant looks really cool when it's "all grown up."

19. Take cheesy Christmas photos.

Get your siblings back together and get Christmas photos done like when you were kids.

20. Treat yourself to a full body massage.

21. Climb to the top of a
          lighthouse.

22. Take down embarrassing pictures you were tagged in online.

It might have been funny at 19 but your new boss may not like that picture of you in a balloon hat with a cigarette hanging from your lips and two forty ounce beers in your hands. Feel free to download them to your computer for private enjoyment though.

23. Splurge on a meal at a really expensive restaurant.

It's totally worth it for the amazing experience of trying gourmet food and the superior service of fine dining.

24. Conquer your stage fright.

Participate in an open mic night and sing your heart out in a cafe.

25. See the ocean.

There is nothing like standing beside the vastness of an ocean to put you into perspective.

26. Learn how to grocery shop on a budget.

It's really hard to eat well without a whole lot of money but it's not impossible. Clip coupons and check the weekly sale ads to see what you can get a good deal on each week. Make a menu of meals and them make a list of what you're getting. The key is to not go to the store without a plan (or hungry!) That's how you end up with a case of beer, a container of Nesquik, and a pound of Cheetos but nothing to actually eat for dinner.

27. Go fishing or crabbing.

Catch your dinner.

28. Ride on a motorcycle.

Please wear a helmet!

29. Become a "regular" somewhere.

Get to know the wait staff at your favorite dive bar or local diner. Return often and tip well. There's nothing better than knowing the people who serve your food at a really good restaurant.

30. Start waking up earlier.

It's fine to sleep in sometimes but don't spend half the day in bed. Having a good morning routine can help improve your life tons (and make waking up on Monday mornings a whole lot easier.)

31. Go to a major sporting event like a championship game.

32. Live in another country.

Many countries offer Visas to young people
for working holidays and tons of young people
choose to do study abroad programs while in their
university's undergraduate program or even a full
master's degree overseas.

33. Throw yourself a huge birthday party.

Whether it's a house party or bringing your friends out to a club, make it a birthday bash to remember.

34. Move out of your parents' house!

This is a huge step in life. Save up the money and get a place of your own or room with some friends from college or shack up with your significant other. Learn to live on your own and enjoy your independence.

35. Go whale watching.

36. Plant a tree.

37. Take a ride in a hot air balloon.

38. Go to a midnight showing of The Rocky Horror Picture Show.

Dressed up, of course.

39. Party for an entire weekend.

You can't party forever so enjoy the easier hangovers while you're young.

40. Play volleyball on a beach.

41. Attend a burlesque show.

42. Race your friends at a go-kart track.

43. Learn another language.

If you didn't exactly master the Spanish language in high school, that's fine. There are tons of apps and programs that are built to help you learn vocabulary and grammar. Check out local meetup groups as well. Many areas have meetups planned for people who are trying to learn a language where locals and native speakers can meetup to practice their speaking skills.

44. Eat whipped cream right from the can.

45. Start telling your parents that you love them.

They won't be around forever. Remind them that you love them, even if you don't like them all the time.

46. Attend a field party.

47. Go a day without wearing shoes.

Feel the ground beneath your feet.

48. Work out four times a week.

Make it a habit. Make it a lifelong habit.

49. Change your hair dramatically.

Dye it a completely different color. Get a pixie cut. Do something new. Hair can always grow back.

50. Learn how to properly put on a condom.

Remember to use one every time.

51. Go horseback riding.

52. Eat dessert for breakfast.

Treat yourself.

53. Make every recipe in a cookbook.

54. Don't be afraid of moving away from your hometown.

There may be better opportunities out there for you so don't limit yourself to the place you've grown up. You can always come back to visit.

55. Take yourself out on a date.

Go out to dinner and a movie alone. Bring along a nice book to read at the table and enjoy treating yourself to something nice.

56. Own a watch.

You shouldn't have to use your cell phone to check the time. You're an adult now. Get a watch. Get a nice watch. Wear it everyday.

57. Swim with dolphins.

58. Write a novel during National Novel Writing Month (NaNoWriMo).

You can do it!

59. Be able to let friendships go.

Sometimes people grow apart, that's a part of life. Learn when you should just let go of an old friendship, whether it's because you've gone down two very different paths in life or perhaps your friend is just a toxic person. Letting go is hard and is a huge step sometimes in the right direction.

60. Go see a Broadway production.

61. Buy a car.

Maybe you've been borrowing your parent's car since you got your licence which isn't a problem when you've just gotten your licence but you're a twenty-something now and it's time to get your own wheels.

62. Apply to be on a reality show.

You only live once, right?

63. Take a bartending class.

Learn to be a cocktail master.

64. Go to a brewery and do a beer tasting.

65. Hike up a mountain.

66. Sleep naked.

Do it at least once. Preferably on a really hot night. There's something really liberating about your bare skin between the sheets. Trust me.

67. Stay up until the early hours of the morning to watch a meteor shower.

68. Grab your passport and visit a foreign country.

Any country. Plan your trip and go. You only have one life so go explore the world you live in and learn about how people in other countries live.

69. When you travel, learn to appreciate the "tourist destinations" but take the time to explore places that aren't "on the map" as well.

90% of the time, you'll have a better experience doing something that wasn't planned or set up just for tourists.

70. Know where the cheapest drinks are in town.

71. Take a dance class.

Salsa, swing, ballet, anything. Get your body moving in new ways.

72. Dance on a bar.

Whether it's your 21st birthday or just another Thursday night, let loose, take that tequila shot you've been avoiding, and hop on the bar. Every once in a while, it's okay to be a little wild.

73. Learn to code and create a website.

It can be a silly blog or something a little more serious but coding is a great skill to know no matter what you do.

74. Jump into a pool/the ocean fully clothed.

75. Donate blood at a
blood drive.

76. Learn your alcohol limit.

It's one thing to be falling down drunk when you're 21. It's a whole other thing to be falling down drunk when you're 25. Learn your limits and stay below them. Everyone will have a better time.

77. Crowd surf at a concert.

78. Get tested regularly for STDs.

Your sexual health is important so be sure to take care of yourself. Women usually can get an STD test whenever they go in for their annual Pap smear.

79. Learn to sew.

Something as simple as sewing on a button and fixing a hemline can come in handy for those moments your coat buttons pop off on your way out of the house before an important meeting.

.

80. Go skinny dipping,

Just do it. (Preferably at a private pool.)

81. Go antiquing and buy something really unique.

82. Learn to do your own laundry.

To be honest, the earlier you learn this the better but it's never too late to learn to sort, wash, dry, and iron.

83. Host a dinner party.

Invite your friends over and cook a big meal for them. It's always fun to have a few laughs over a good, home cooked meal. (And it's cheaper than going out as well!)

84. Learn to use a fire extinguisher.

It's better to learn before you need to know how to use one.

85. Ride the biggest roller coaster at the theme park.

Scream until your throat hurts.

86. Learn to seek help.

If you've got problem, especially a mental or physical health problem, learn to ask for help when you need it. Call a help line or talk to a doctor or a trusted family member who can help you. It doesn't make you any less of an adult for needing help when you're struggling.

87. Be up against the rail or front row at a concert.

88. Finish a whole tube
of chapstick before
losing it.

89. Go to an orchard and pick your own fruit.

Then go home and bake a pie or cobbler with it.

90. Buy a pair of jumper cables, learn to use them, and then throw them in your trunk.

You never know when you'll accidentally leave your headlights on all night and need a jump to get to work or school the next day.

91. Meet a celebrity.

92. Go to 10 cent wing night at the local sports bar and eat your weight in wings.

93. Dress up and go out to eat at a nice restaurant.

You know, a really nice restaurant with white tablecloths and candles on the table. Everyone deserves to spend a little extra money on a really awesome meal every now and then.

94. Learn to budget.

Sure it's fun wondering if your card is going to be declined every time you buy a sandwich at the deli when you're younger. Now, it's just getting irresponsible (and expensive--those overdraft fees!) Start budgeting and tracking your spending. Your wallet will thank you.

95. Learn to say "It's my fault."

Owning up to your actions (even if it was a mistake) is always better than lying about them. Learn to be the bigger person and admit fault.

96. Take a first aid course.

The Red Cross usually offers them year-round in most places and for relatively cheap. You never know when your first aid could save someone's life.

97. Have a drink out of a real coconut.

98. Trace your family history and learn where you came from.

99. Get your palm read.

It'll be silly and will probably cost $5-$10 but why not?

100. Register to vote and then go do it!

There's a huge drive to get young people to vote and guess what, that means you. Your vote is your voice so use it.

101. Start a windowsill garden for herbs or flowers.

Something small to brighten your day.

102. Travel solo.

It might seem terrifying to go somewhere all on your own but spending quality time with yourself in somewhere completely new is a unique and exciting experience everyone should have before turning 25.

103. Win a giant stuffed animal playing a carnival game.

104. Make jello shots.

I recommend using a turkey baster to fill your little cups to avoid covering your kitchen in sticky, alcoholic liquid gelatin.

105. Run a 5k.

106. Learn one of your grandma's recipes so you can pass it down to your kids/grandkids.

107. Have a "craft day" with your friends and DIY some new decorations for your apartments/ houses.

Moving out and decorating can be expensive for someone in their early 20s so DIY can be the difference between a sad piece of thrift store furniture and something that looks expensive and unique.

108. Open a savings
account and put at least
$20 in it a month.

109. Learn to swim.

110. Watch the top 100 movies of all time.

111. Make a piece of art to hang in your living room.

112. Own a toolkit.

You're probably going to have to fix things every
now and then and having the right tools for the job
is important. Put together a toolbox for yourself.

113. Learn to say no. You don't have to do everything people ask you to do.

Learn when to say know and your life can really improve drastically.

114. On the other hand, learn to say yes as well.

Sometimes we miss out on important moments in life because we're afraid. Sometimes, you just need to say yes. Say yes to new things, new people, and new adventures. Don't miss out because you're nervous or timid. Choose to put yourself out there more often and gain some new experiences.

115. Make your own smoothies.

All you need is a blender, ice, fruit, juices or yogurt and some sugar or artificial sweetener for a cool yummy treat.

116. Bake a cake from scratch.

Break out the cookbooks, no box mixes allowed!

117. Accept that the older you get, the worse your hangovers get.

118. Spend a whole day on the beach.

119. Wash your sheets regularly.

Clean sheets are good for your skin and are just generally hygienic. Wash them.

120. Stop worrying if you haven't found the right guy or girl for you.

Seriously, you have your whole life to figure that out; you don't need to get married or engaged right out of college. You've got tons of other cool stuff to do first so don't worry if Mr. or Mrs. Right hasn't found you yet.

121. Do a "30 day challenge."

Whether it's going vegetarian, cleaning your house, getting in shape, or any other goal you have, take a challenge to accomplish your goal in 30 days.

122. Get CPR certified.

It's better to be trained and never need to use it than to be untrained in an emergency situation.

123. Attend a fashion show.

124. Get something waxed.

Whether it's your eyebrows, upper lip, or bikini line, get something waxed at least once.

125. Go to a music festival.

You're only young once. So go to a music festival, camp out, get dirty, drink too much, and enjoy the bands.

126. Start recycling items in your home or school if you don't already.

Create a place for recyclable items to be stored, find out where they need to be taken or if they can be picked up, and figure out what items you can recycle.

127. Start (and stick to) a skincare routine.

Wash your face before bed and remember to moisturize, at the minimum.

128. Learn to change a tire and keep a spare in your car.

No matter how small your car is, make room for a spare tire!

129. Fall in love.

130. See your favorite band in concert.

131. Learn to tie a tie.

132. Marathon an entire
TV series one weekend.

133. Paint an entire room.

Sometimes a new coat of paint is all a place needs to look like a million bucks.

134. Take your parents out to dinner.

A simple gesture of just taking them out (and picking up the bill) is a simple way to show your parents you appreciate what they've done for you.

135. Take a mental health day.

Don't make it a habit but the occasional day off to do nothing is totally fine.

136. Go to a wine and cheese tasting.

Dress up a bit, schmooze with some other classy people, and learn how to pair wines and cheeses together to bring out the flavors. It's amazing what a good wine/cheese pairing will do to your tastebuds.

137. Know how to set a formal dinner table.

Yes, with all of those forks and spoons.)

138. Pay off your entire credit card bill.

139. Master a handshake.

No one likes a limp handshake so learn the art of a good, firm handshake.

140. Gamble at a casino.

141. Pose for an art class.

142. Own an alarm clock.

Don't rely on your cell phone to wake you up.
Sometimes you just need a good old fashion alarm
clock to wake you from your gentle slumber and get
you to work on time.

143. Publish an eBook.

It's really easy to publish a book on Amazon now so write a book about something you're passionate about and earn the title of "published author."

144. Create your own signature drink.

145. Drink a glass of real champagne.

146. Get up on stage and perform at a karaoke bar.

It's totally fine if you need a drink or two first!

147. Attend a book signing for your favorite author.

148. Learn to make the perfect cup of coffee.

149. Buy an "investment piece" for your wardrobe.

You don't need to drop $3,000 but investing in a good pair of shoes or a nice handbag that you'll use for years is a worthwhile expense.

150. Learn how to ask for a raise.

Sometimes just asking in a polite yet assertive way is just the push your boss needs to give you an extra $1000 a year.

151. Participate in trivia or quiz night at a local bar.

You'll get to test the knowledge you've learned and enjoy the drink specials. Two birds with one stone!

152. Go star gazing.

Drive somewhere out into the country that there
aren't many lights or light pollution to cover
the stars. Bring a star map and map out the
constellations or just lay out a blanket and look up
at the universe. If it's a really clear night and there's
not a lot of light, you might even be able to see the
Milky Way.

153. Visit a Disney Theme Park.

154. Go to a comic book convention in full cosplay.

155. Get a real manicure/ pedicure.

156. Go on a roadtrip.

Whether it's a day trip or a week long adventure, plan it out, save up some money and make it a reality.

157. Learn to juggle.

Or learn a different "party trick" that is simple and yet impressive to a group of semi-drunk people.

158. Participate in a protest.

Figure out what you believe in and stand up for it.

159. Own a piece of furniture that didn't come from a thrift store or a family member.

160. Attend a midnight movie release.

161. Visit a haunted house.

162. Go skiing or
snowboarding in the
mountains.

163. Learn to introduce yourself to other people.

You'll never meet anyone new if you can't say hello.

164. Attend a political event or rally and support your favorite candidate.

165. Go see a ballet performance.

166. Start regularly donating to charity.

Even if it's just $10 a month or so, a regular contribution to your favorite charity can go a long way.

167. Get something pierced.

Even if it's just your ears.

168. Eat an exotic meat dish.

Such as alligator, kangaroo, or ostrich.

169. Write a song.

170. Conquer your fear of needles and get acupuncture.

171. Get a tattoo.

172. Go out for a big
boozy brunch with
friends.

173. Give back by volunteering for a Habitat for Humanity build (or another charity that does similar work in your country.)

174. Take an improv class.

175. Shoot a gun.

Whether it's going to a gun range to shoot a handgun or using a rifle to go clay pigeon shooting, give it a go.

176. Perfect your resume.

177. Learn to drive a stick shift.

You never know when you'll need to drive a friend's car home for some reason and lo and behold... it's a manual.

178. Grow your hair out
to donate it to children
with cancer.

179. Get a credit card and learn to use it responsibly.

180. Travel and stay in a very low budget hotel or hostel.

181. Learn to play poker
and have a poker night
with your friends.

182. Visit an aquarium.

183. Go on a city-wide scavenger hunt.

184. Start a personal library.

A house without books is a sad house. Surround yourself with books. It helps if you read them too.

185. Know how to prepare
eggs in at least two ways.

186. Do a flaming shot.

You should probably do this one at a bar (under supervision) and pretty early in the night.

187. Start expanding your palate.

If you've been a picky eater all your life, now is your time to start exploring different food.

188. Have a positive attitude.

It's amazing how much changing your attitude can really change your life and improve your friendships and even your grades. Just try to think a little more positively each day.

189. Learn to play an instrument.

190. Go see your favorite sports team play at their home stadium.

191. Learn to disconnect.

You don't need to check your Facebook every two seconds to find out if someone you knew back in high school is having another baby or your distant cousin is having a birthday. Learn to put down your phone and enjoy life outside of the internet for a bit.

192. Have a bonfire on a cold night.

Invite your friends, bundle up, have a few beers and roast some marshmallows.

193. Read 52 books in 52 weeks (that's 1 book a week for a whole year!)

194. Quit a bad habit.

Biting your nails? Smoking? Leaving your clothes on the floor? Change it!

195. Buy a lottery ticket.

196. Volunteer for a
local charity or non-
profit organization that
you care about.

197. View a total eclipse.

Solar, lunar, or heart.

198. Throw a house party.

This is no dinner party. Break out the booze and maybe a few bowls of chips and crank up the music. Invite everyone you know and have a awesome party.

199. Do all of the tourist-y things in your hometown.

200. Do a 365 photo project.

201. Stop being embarrassed about buying tampons, condoms, anti-diarrhea medication at the pharmacy.

It's a fact of life.

202. Get backstage at a concert.

203. Buy something luxurious and expensive just because you want it.

Sometimes you just need to treat yourself to something special whether you really *need* it or not.

204. Host a holiday meal for your family, friends, or both!

205. Spend an afternoon walking through a museum on your own.

Going to a museum on your own means you can spend as much time as you want reading and looking over the things you find most interesting. It's a quiet place to contemplate life, art, and history.

206. Go to the zoo to see
your favorite animals.

207. Make your favorite
dessert from scratch.

208. Try new foods.

Whether it's sushi or maybe you've just never had a taste for pizza, learn to try things, even if you already think you don't like them.

209. Fly somewhere in
          airplane.

210. Start planning ahead for things.

There's nothing worse than being on the way to a birthday party and still needing to stop and buy a card. Start planning ahead. Keep a calendar and schedule time to catch up on things you need to do like buying gifts or mailing a thank you note.

211. Stop using wire hangers and do something nice for your clothes by buying better hangers.

212. Make your own
homemade pickles or jam
to can and give away to
friends and family.

213. Participate in a flash mob.

214. Have a "no spend" month where you don't buy anything frivolous such as new clothes, shoes, or books for a whole month.

It's a good way to start a savings and show how much you buy on impulse.

215. Go out to eat and don't read the description of what you're ordering.

Just point at something on the menu and be surprised with what the waiter brings to the table.

216. Dress up and participate in a Zombie Walk.

Brains!

217. Get your heart broken.

Heartbreak sucks. It sucks a lot. But it's how you learn to move on and deal with change.

218. Donate to a Kickstarter campaign and be a part of something new.

219. Go on a camping trip with your friends.

220. Be able to do 20 consecutive real push-ups.

221. Conquer your fears and go skydiving.

222. Send Christmas cards.

Even if it's a cheesy picture of you and your cat in front of the Christmas tree, send some cards to your friends and family and spread some holiday cheer. It's an "adult" thing to do that reminds people you're thinking about them during the holidays.

223. Read that really
long book you've been
      meaning to read.

224. Attend a murder mystery dinner.

They are hilarious and super fun as long as everyone is game to be in character.

225. Have an entirely DIY holiday season.

Meaning you will make all of the gifts you give out. This can be anything from baking tins of cookies to give out or knitting everyone hat and scarf sets. Either way, a little handmade love goes a long way.

226. Learn not to over react.

Sometimes it's easy to get upset over something but remaining calm and keeping your head can really help in a time of stress.

227. Spend an evening with your friends at a rooftop bar.

228. Start meditating.

A few minutes of quiet mindfulness a day can g a
long way toward your mental and emotional health.

229. Buy a pedometer.

Aim to walk 10,000 steps per day.

230. Do at least 5 projects you've pinned on Pinterest.

No more saying "I'll get around to it one of these days."

231. Spend a day canoeing down a river with a few friends.

232. Stop putting off doctor/dentist appointments and just go.

Take care of yourself.

233. Start actually eating breakfast.

It's the most important meal of the day so why are you just eating a burnt piece of toast or a sugar coated granola bar on the train to work?

234. Have afternoon tea somewhere fancy.

235. Go nude on a nude beach.

You're only young once.

236. Sit up straight.

Poor posture can make you look and feel uncomfortable. Be conscious when your shoulders start to slouch and pull them back.

237. Watch the sun rise and set over the ocean.

238. Take a spontaneous trip somewhere.

Wake up, get dressed, and get out the door. Go somewhere new whether it's nearby or across the country.

239. Join the bone marrow
registry and potentially
save a life.

240. Go to a professional conference.

241. Restore a piece of furniture.

Maybe you've got a desk you *love* but it needs some TLC or your mom gave you a really comfy chair but the fabric on it is just… meh. Take that old furniture up a notch a restore it.

242. Have your own business cards.

Even if you're just starting out, having a business card to give away can do wonders for you professionally because the people you meet will have a little something to remember you by. You can print your own if your company doesn't provide them for you.

243. Smile more.

Just the act of smiling can make you look and feel
happier and more confident.

244. Go on a picnic in the park with friends.

245. Go to an outdoor movie or theatre performance.

246. Be in a wedding.

By 25, you're bound to know at least a handful of people who are getting/have gotten married. Being in someone's wedding is a fun experience that allows you to meet new people such as their bridesmaids or groomsmen and lets you bond with your friend, the bride or groom-to-be even more.

247. Order room service.

248. Clean out your closet.

Get rid of those clothes you never ever wear and make room for stuff you actually will wear and like.

249. Be more decisive.

No more "I don't know, what do you want to do?"
Learn to speak up and say what you want.

250. Write a letter to yourself to read on your 30th birthday.

Fill it with the things you think you'd have accomplished by then and where you hope to be.

More Books By Tammy Mitchell

The Teenage Bucket List: 250 Things To Do Before You Turn 18

The College Bucket List: 250 Things to Do Before You Finish College

Booze Free Fridays: 200 Things To Do In College Without Drinking

365 Days of Dates

250 Things To Do With Your BFF

29315589R00151

Printed in Great Britain
by Amazon